A WORLD AFTER...

# FOSSIL FUELS

Liz Gogerly

Heinemann
LIBRARY

Chicago, Illinois

Edited by Andrew Farrow, Adrian Vigliano,
  and Vaarunika Dharmapala
Designed by Philippa Jenkins
Original illustrations © Capstone Global Library
  Limited 2013
Illustrated by HL Studios and Alvaro Fernandez
  Villa Advocate-Art pp4-5
Picture research by Mica Brancic
Printed and bound in China

17 16 15 14 13
10 9 8 7 6 5 4 3 2 1

**Library of Congress Cataloging-in-
Publication Data**
Gogerly, Liz.
  Fossil fuels / Liz Gogerly.
     p. cm.—(A world after)
  Includes bibliographical references and
index.
  ISBN 978-1-4329-7619-4 (hb)—ISBN 978-1-
4329-7624-8 (pb)  1. Energy security—Juvenile
literature. 2. Fossil fuels—Juvenile literature. 3.
Petroleum reserves—Forecasting—Juvenile
literature.  I. Title.

  HD9502.A2G64 2014
  333.8'2—dc23                    2012035007

**Acknowledgments**
We would like to thank the following for
permission to reproduce photographs: Alamy
pp 11 (© Art Directors & TRIP), 12 (© Everyday
Images), 16 (© JFP), 19 (© epa european
pressphoto agency b.v.), 26 (© AF archive),
31 (© PhotoStock-Israel/Asaf Sultan), 41 (©
Thomas Jackson); Corbis pp 14 (VII/© Ashley
Gilbertson), 15 (Demotix/© Tom Craig), 18
(epa/© Juan Carlos Hidalgo), 24 (© Ashley
Cooper), 29 (© Frans Lanting), 33 (Demotix/©
Majdi Fathi), 34 (epa/© Piyal Adhikary), 40
(imagebroker/© Daniel Schoenen), 44 (Dagens
Naringsliv/© Orjan F. Ellingvag), 46 (Blend
Images/© KidStock); Getty Images pp 7 (Time
& Life Pictures/Allan Tannenbaum), 20 (AFP/
Marc Hofer), 21 (AFP/Adek Berry), 23 (Matthew
Peyton), 39 (Robert Nickelsberg); Press
Association p 43 (AP Photo/Josh Reynolds);
Reuters p 25 (Dave Amit); Science Photo
Library p 47 (Detlev Van Ravensway).

Design features throughout courtesy of
Shutterstock: empty cork bulletin board,
background (© Reinhold Leitner), storm
clouds (© KavardakovA), chain link fence
(© ARENA Creative).

Cover photograph of a pile of used cars
reproduced with permission of Shutterstock
(© Fortish).

We would like to thank Michael Mastrandrea
for his invaluable help in the preparation of
this book.

Every effort has been made to contact
copyright holders of material reproduced
in this book. Any omissions will be rectified
in subsequent printings if notice is given to
the publisher.

**Disclaimer**
All the Internet addresses (URLs) given in this
book were valid at the time of going to press.
However, due to the dynamic nature of the
Internet, some addresses may have changed,
or sites may have changed or ceased to exist
since publication. While the author and
publisher regret any inconvenience this may
cause readers, no responsibility for any such
changes can be accepted by either the author
or the publisher.

# CONTENTS

Some words are printed in bold, **like this**. You can find out
what they mean by looking in the glossary.

# PROLOGUE

March 20, 2020

Four days ago, terrorists set off a series of car bombs near government buildings in the Saudi capital, Riyadh. In the following days, suicide bombers took out homes and other places that are popular with Westerners living in the city. Yesterday, two trucks packed with explosives forced their way into the Saudis' biggest oil refinery and destroyed it. This morning, there are reports of terrorist attacks on oil tankers passing through the Persian Gulf.

THE SITUATION IS SERIOUS, AS ABOUT 40 PERCENT OF THE WORLD'S TRADED OIL PASSES THROUGH THE GULF.

GOVERNMENTS ARE URGING PEOPLE NOT TO PANIC.

I guess I should probably get to the gas station and fill up with gasoline right now.

I blame the terrorists for this mess!

We've been lining up for hours. Hope the gas doesn't run out.

Can't help but feel panicked!

# THE WORLD WAKES UP

If there were a serious and long-term disruption to oil supplies in the Middle East, how would it affect us? What would the world be like without enough fossil fuels? The story you are about to read is just one idea of how things might develop as a result of this situation. No one can know for sure how the world will cope as we run out of fossil fuels, and things could turn out very differently.

After reports of trouble in the Middle East in 2020, the first reaction is concern about gasoline. News alerts on television, radio, and the Internet about the terrorist attacks in the Persian Gulf make everyone think about the effect on fuel supplies. The headlines provoke anxiety. Although there is no immediate fuel shortage, lines begin to form at gas stations around the world, as people rush out to fill up their tanks. In 2020, people have a different mindset from us today. They are more aware that world oil supplies are running out. The terrorist attacks in the Middle East force them to pay attention to a crisis that had been looming for a long time.

## Searching for solutions

Behind the scenes, world leaders work toward a solution. They conduct emergency meetings to make backup plans. Talks with the leaders of **OPEC (Organization of the Petroleum Exporting Countries)** are at the top of the agenda. Chief executives of multinational fuel companies are hauled into meetings to discuss oil reserves and how to manage the crisis. There is panic among many leaders, but politicians tell the public to keep calm. However, it is only a matter of time before people question the leaders' power to solve this massive problem…

### WHAT WOULD YOU DO?

**Buying fuel**

In an oil crisis, would you rush out to buy fuel? Would you listen to the news and join the panic, or would you remain calm and think that your government will get the situation under control?

# HOW LIKELY IS IT?

## A sudden world oil crisis

In 1973, Americans were confronted with a serious oil crisis. It began with the 1973 Arab-Israeli War, also known as the Yom Kippur War.

Fighting between Israel and a coalition of Egypt and Syria began in October 1973. The Arab members of OPEC declared an oil embargo (banned the trade of oil) on the United States when it re-supplied the Israeli military. Between October 1973 and March 1974, Arab oil producers ceased to supply oil to the United States. The embargo was later extended to other Western countries and to Japan. The Arab nations wanted to put pressure on the United States to withhold support from the Israelis.

### Emergency measures

The U.S. government, under President Richard Nixon, did not give in to the Arab nations' demands, and the United States was plunged into an oil crisis.

Huge lines at gas stations became normal. Within a month, the price of gasoline quadrupled. People attempted to cut their consumption of oil. Nixon requested that gas stations stop selling gasoline on Saturday nights and Sundays. Together with emergency measures, such as lowering the speed limit to 55 miles (88 kilometers) per hour, Americans managed to lower oil consumption by about 20 percent. Rationing was under consideration, but the crisis ended before it could be put in place.

Once the embargo was lifted, the price of fuel fell, and people returned to their everyday lives. However, long-term effects of the crisis in the United States include the production of more fuel-efficient cars and oil heating being gradually replaced by electric heating.

↗ These cars are lining up for gasoline in January 1974, during an oil crisis that happened then.

# An oil crisis of the future

The 1973 oil crisis lasted about six months. The oil crisis in 2020 is about to set the world in turmoil. In 2020, the challenge is dealing with an oil crisis at a time when there is less oil overall.

For many years, experts, especially **geologists**, have warned about a time when oil production will go into decline. This means that the amount of oil that is extracted each day will go down and the cost of oil will go up. They predict that the decline in oil will occur after we have reached "peak oil." Peak oil is the time when oil production is at its highest. Some experts believe that once we have reached peak oil, we have about 20 years before supplies run out. However, nobody knows for sure. In the year 2020, discussions about an impending oil crisis are regularly in the news. People quickly realize that this situation is going to be very serious.

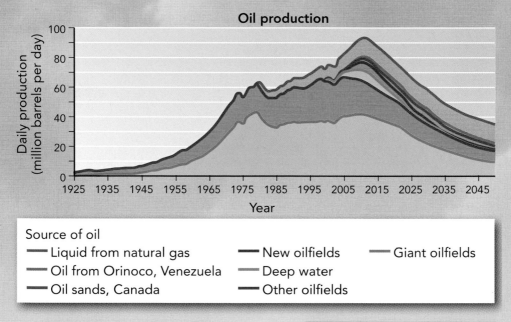

## Oil production

Source of oil
- Liquid from natural gas
- Oil from Orinoco, Venezuela
- Oil sands, Canada
- New oilfields
- Deep water
- Other oilfields
- Giant oilfields

## The domino effect

In the future, it may be a wave of terrorist bombs or a natural disaster that triggers an energy crisis. Panic at the gas pumps would be the first symptom of the crisis. Rising transportation costs would affect food distribution. Inevitably, stores and businesses would close. So much of modern society is based on burning oil that it is not difficult to see how an oil crisis could escalate into a full-scale crisis.

This graph shows estimated world oil production from 1925 to 2045. According to this projection, we reached peak oil in about 2010, and oil production is now in decline.

Scientists cannot accurately predict when peak oil will happen. Matthew Simmons, author of a 2005 book called *Twilight in the Desert: The Coming Saudi Oil Shock and the World Economy*, suggests: "Peaking is one of these fuzzy events that you only know clearly when you see it through a rear view mirror, and by then an alternate resolution is generally too late."

Some experts think that we reached the peak of easy-to-drill **crude oil** in 2004. Others have estimated it could be any time between 2006 and 2016. Reaching peak oil does not mean the end of oil supplies, but it leads to an age when there will not be enough oil to meet demand, a situation that will cause further fuel inflation.

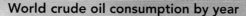

## World crude oil consumption by year

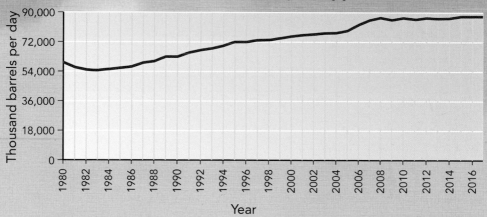

# Crisis management

How well we would really cope with such a situation in the future depends upon what happens in the world between now and when (and if) a crisis occurs. On the positive side, scientists have been coming up with alternatives to petroleum-based fuels for decades. In 2011, annual oil demand in the United States actually fell. However, global demand for oil continued to rise, especially in newly industrialized nations such as China and India.

This diagram shows that oil consumption has steadily increased from the mid-1980s to 2012. The world could survive a fuel crisis in the future if demand for oil fell in line with the supply of oil.

## Balance of power

As we have seen, meetings between world leaders and major oil companies are focused on handling the situation. Another important matter they look at is oil reserves. Oil reserves are the estimated quantity of crude oil that can be extracted in a way that meets commercial needs. Saudi Arabia has the largest proven oil reserves in the world, followed by Venezuela, Canada, Iran, Iraq, and Kuwait. Since most of the oil reserves in the world are in the Middle East, a terrorist situation in that area has a dramatic effect on Western industrial nations. Industry is dependent on crude oil. Even a short-term disruption to oil supplies has the power to damage the world's major economies.

## PRODUCTS MADE FROM OIL

- gasoline
- plastics
- solvents
- cosmetics
- drugs
- paint
- detergents
- ink
- pesticides
- fabric

Ordinary people want answers about what is going to happen next. Many question the importance of oil and whether other fossil fuels can be utilized in the crisis. In the year 2020, people are more aware of the **scarcity** of fossil fuels. They understand there is a connection between fossil fuels and climate change. They are anxious about environmental issues, but since the **Industrial Revolution**, fossil fuels have played a major part in our lives, to a point where we have become dependent on them.

## Fossil fuel facts

The world's fossil fuels include coal, oil, and natural gas. These are made from the fossilized remains of prehistoric plants and animals. They were formed millions of years ago and usually need to be extracted from underground. They are called **nonrenewable resources** because they are produced naturally only at a very slow rate and so cannot be replaced. Coal has been used for heat and cooking for thousands of years, and deposits can be found all around the world. Coal powered the Industrial Revolution.

However, as important as coal has been in the industrialization of the world, it is not a good oil replacement. Coal can be turned into a gasoline-like fuel for vehicles, but the process for making this fuel uses a lot of energy. Coal also emits up to twice the amount of **carbon dioxide** as oil, which means it contributes more to **global warming**. One day, coal will also run out. Some scientists think global peak coal may take place in about 200 years.

# NATURAL GAS

Natural gas is another fossil fuel that has been used since ancient times. Natural gas vehicles (NGVs) can run on liquefied natural gas (LNG) or compressed natural gas (CNG). In 2010, there were about 12.67 million NGVs on the road and 18,200 filling stations worldwide. Natural gas contributes less to global warming, so in theory it is a good replacement for oil. However, there is the question of peak gas. In 2008, the U.S. Energy Information Administration predicted growth until 2030, after which natural gas production may go into decline.

This is an oil refinery in Saudi Arabia. Some experts predict that Saudi Arabia will reach peak oil in the near future.

# Fuel theft

At the start of the oil crisis, the first people to feel the pinch are the less wealthy. Despite fuel inflation, the wealthy can afford to fuel their vehicles. As the days go by, the economic divide adds to the tension. Today, in the United States and other countries, there have been reports of fuel theft in recent years. Thieves have cut through fuel lines, broken open fuel caps, removed gas tanks, or used pumping equipment to steal gasoline. In 2020, the rise in fuel theft is blamed on the rising cost of gasoline.

Within weeks, gasoline becomes so scarce and expensive that fuel theft is an everyday occurrence. The streets are a danger zone where armed thieves look for easy targets. Cars parked on the road are like sitting ducks. Fuel tanks left unguarded can be easily plundered. Some thieves steal to satisfy their own needs. Organized groups steal in bulk to supply the **black market**. Anyone with a full tank of fuel needs to be security conscious and vigilant at all times.

How low will people go in a crisis? Stealing gasoline from another car is quick and easy and becomes more commonplace as desperation sets in.

# Protest on the streets

Panic leads to protest. Many people vent their frustration at rising fuel costs by holding protest marches. Much of their anger is directed at the governments of the world. Around the globe, groups of protesters form outside government buildings. In the past, these kinds of protests were generally against rising fuel costs or to voice concerns about the environment. Now, people are pleading for more oil. There are scenes of chaos and confusion. Protesting does not bring them the answers or results they need. There is a rising feeling of unrest, instability, helplessness, and impending doom.

## HOW LIKELY IS IT?

### A fuel panic

In March 2012, the United Kingdom experienced a fuel panic that had the potential to bring the nation to a standstill. Since 2000, a series of fuel protests have taken place in the country in response to rising fuel costs. In 2005, protests resulted in some panic buying on the part of the public. However, panic buying in 2012 occurred as a result of the mere threat of a protest by gasoline tanker drivers. Their dispute was over working conditions and employment contracts; there was no shortage of fuel, and a strike had not been organized.

The panic started when government minister Francis Maude told the public they should have full tanks of gasoline and "maybe a little in their garage as well in a [gas] can." Thousands of drivers rushed to gas stations to fill up, even though it would be many days before a strike could begin.

Within days, gasoline sales rose by 170 percent. All over the country, stations ran dry. There were scenes of "fuel rage" as people got angry with each other at gas stations. The army was put on standby in case there was a national emergency. The strike never went ahead, but this fuel crisis demonstrated how quickly people could be panicked into buying fuel they did not immediately need.

# PANIC SETS IN

By the second week of the crisis, the reality has hit home for millions of people. There is less traffic on the roads. Many people have stopped using their cars because they cannot afford to fill them up with gasoline or **diesel**. By 2020, there are more vehicles using **biofuel** and electric cars. There are also some magnetically controlled cars and cars run on compressed air. However, these are expensive, and most people have not made the switch to this new technology. In the past, biofuel was praised as the replacement for gasoline and diesel. Now, it is clear that the world has not done enough to make the transition to biofuels.

Many people have started to accept that life is not going to return to normal. Millions of people who usually use their cars to get to work are stranded at home. Meanwhile, some people have become more resourceful. A group of New York commuters has set up a web site to promote car sharing. The idea is catching on everywhere. More people are getting on their bikes again. Sales of bicycles have skyrocketed; in some places, the only way you will get a new bike is on the black market.

The 2003 oil crisis in Iraq meant fuel prices increased and rationing had to be introduced. Lines of over a mile were reported at some gas stations.

## HOW LIKELY IS IT?
### Can we make biofuels from seaweed?

Biofuels are produced from **renewable resources** such as plant **biomass**, vegetable oils, and waste materials. Bioethanol is made from crops such as corn or sugarcane and is currently the most commonly available biofuel worldwide. Biodiesel is produced from vegetable oils and animal fats. In 2011, scientists at the Bio Architecture Lab in California made a breakthrough in microbe research that allowed them to convert seaweed to ethanol. Biofuel from seaweed could help to solve a future oil crisis. Seaweed is fast-growing and plentiful in coastal areas. At the moment, the processing of seaweed to ethanol is expensive. Ben Graziano of the Carbon Trust believes that seaweed could be a great alternative to other biofuels, saying: "The potential is certainly there, not least because most of the Earth is covered in water. If they can get the scale up and the costs down, it has huge potential."

By 2020, there may be more cars like this Renault electric micro car—but will they survive an oil crisis any better than cars that use gasoline?

## Electric cars at a standstill

All around the world, there is an increase in carjackings. Expensive electric cars are the most vulnerable. Electric car owners have become more cautious and are scared to go out in their vehicles. As the fuel crisis continues, it is apparent just how reliant these so-called environmentally friendly cars are on fossil fuels, too. Until recently, replacement engine parts for electric cars were delivered by trucks run on diesel. Now that the price of diesel has quadrupled, the trucks are not making the deliveries. It is only a matter of time before the electric car is grounded, too.

# Stores run dry

Fewer trucks means that the delivery of all supplies is breaking down. Panic buying of all commodities is adding to the crisis. Staples such as bread, dairy products, fresh fruits and vegetables, and toiletries are flying off the supermarket shelves. Shipments of food from around the world are severely affected, and imported goods are incredibly expensive. Some governments are imposing emergency measures such as rationing to ensure the fair distribution of food, clothes, and other goods. Looting and theft are on the increase. The U.S. government has been forced to introduce **curfews** to maintain public order. In Italy, the army has fired water cannons to break up a huge crowd of desperate, angry people who had lined up unsuccessfully to buy bread.

Empty supermarket shelves mean many people struggle to feed themselves during the crisis.

## WHAT WOULD YOU DO?

### Stocking up on food

What would you do if your local supermarkets did not have any more fresh fruits and vegetables? Perhaps you would seek out locally grown food? How long would it be before you decided you would have to start growing your own food?

## TOILET PAPER RUNS OUT

In 1973, during the oil crisis in the United States, people began buying toilet paper after a comedian on television joked that there would be a shortage. On this occasion, it was people's panic buying that actually caused the shortage. Normal delivery of toilet paper resumed after a few weeks.

## FACT OR FICTION?

**Ghost town**

"Lyndhurst was a ghost town, almost. There were no money-bringing tourists now, and the Forest [the New Forest], wilder than before, did not provide enough income to support a community. They boomed down deserted streets, left and left again. An old man leaning on a staff watching sheep graze a stretch of close-nibbled common [land] turned at the sound of the motor, shook his fist at them and shouted something indistinguishable. But a curse, for certain."

Taken from *The Changes: The Weathermonger* by Peter Dickinson (Victor Gollancz, 1968). The novel is about a country that has been forced back to a medieval way of life, where machines are seen as the enemy.

# Small businesses shut down

Towns and cities throughout the world are quieter and scarier places. There is an ever-present danger of being mugged or having a bag of precious food being snatched by thieves. There is less traffic and many more pedestrians and people are using their bicycles. However, everyone seems to be in a rush to get home to safety. The old and sick have retreated inside and rely upon others to help them. Small businesses such as coffee shops, bars, and stores are closing down. Boarded-up businesses add to the general air of doom and gloom. In places like the United States and Australia, many remote towns and regions have become cut off from the rest of the country. Some places are being abandoned altogether to become ghost towns.

# Chaos in the skies

The oil crisis has an immediate effect on the airline industry. In 2010, the shutting down of airspace over northern Europe (see box below) caused widespread chaos. This crisis lasted for six days, but in a world suffering from an oil crisis, the situation is more serious. Flights all around the world are canceled. In 2020, some airlines have alternative renewable jet fuels (see box, opposite), but most have not made a full transition. At first, there are chaotic scenes at airports, as stranded travelers try to make their way home. Within days, nonemergency flights are subject to cancellation or delay. Within weeks, trade, tourism, and other businesses are severely affected.

## HOW LIKELY IS IT?

### Would a crisis in air travel affect the world economy?

In April 2010, Iceland's Eyjafjallajökull's volcano erupted, creating an ash cloud that covered parts of northern Europe. Although the eruption was relatively small, it caused the largest shutdown of air traffic since World War II (1939–1945). The fine, sharp ash particles posed a safety risk to aircraft, so airspace was closed for six days across much of Europe. Over 100,000 flights were canceled and, according to the International Air Transport Association (IATA), the airline industry lost $1.7 billion.

Millions of passengers struggled to find alternative ways to get home. International trade was also affected, especially the transportation of perishable goods such as vegetables and flowers. Many economies around the world suffered as a consequence. African exporters of green beans alone lost an estimated $3.9 million because of the shutdown! Now, imagine the scene in 2020, when the disruption would last much longer than six days. The effect on the world economy would be enormous.

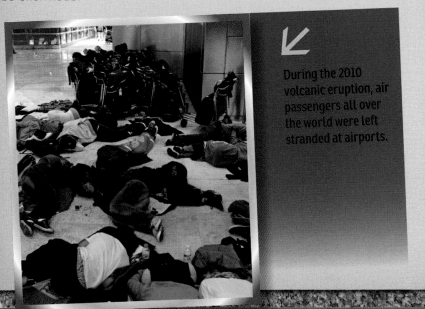

During the 2010 volcanic eruption, air passengers all over the world were left stranded at airports.

# HOW LIKELY IS IT?

## Jet fuel from waste

Biofuel produced from waste is another potential solution for our energy needs in the future. Organic waste, such as rotting food, goes into landfill and gives off a gas called methane or landfill gas. Methane is a greenhouse gas that contributes to global warming. Serious research into utilizing these gases began in the 1970s. Rather than sending garbage off to landfill, the waste can be converted to gas or fuel in machines called **anaerobic digesters**.

In 2012, British Airways announced its plans to convert the garbage of the residents of London into jet fuel. The first plant is expected to open in 2015. The aim is to turn about half a million tons of household waste into about 50,000 tons of jet fuel every year. This would provide only about 2 percent of the airline's current fuel needs, but if it is successful, the airline proposes to extend the project.

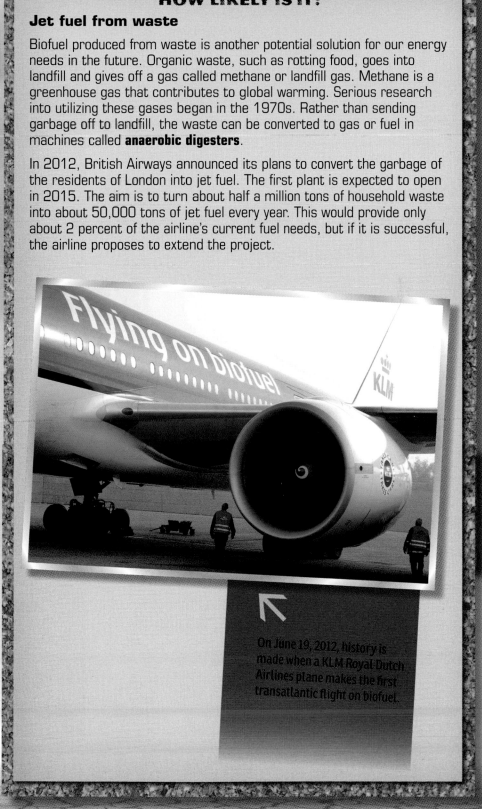

On June 19, 2012, history is made when a KLM Royal Dutch Airlines plane makes the first transatlantic flight on biofuel.

# Mass transit meltdown

By 2020, many rail networks around the world are still using electric and diesel locomotives. Diesel locomotives are used for pulling freight and passenger trains. The rising cost of diesel followed by shortages of fuel mean that many of these services are canceled. The crisis also affects the power supply. Power outages mean electric locomotives are unreliable. Rail passengers are getting frustrated with the limited services available. The lucky few who manage to get on trains have to pay highly inflated fares.

At cargo stations everywhere, undelivered cargo is piling high. The stench from perishable goods that have started to rot is disgusting. At night, thieves steal from the containers. Fewer supplies are reaching the consumers in towns and cities. In the 19th century, the railroad revolutionized travel. In 2020, the crippled rail system is a massive wake-up call to everyone. People living in remote towns and cities feel more cut off than ever, while people living in urban areas feel there is no way out.

*"Back in 1989 I became deeply depressed when I concluded that our greatest scientific achievements will soon be forgotten and our most cherished moments will crumble to dust. But more so, I knew that my children would feel the pressure, and will likely suffer. That really hurt...."*

Richard Duncan, the Institute of Energy and Man, taken from *The Party's Over: Oil, War and the Fate of Industrial Societies* by Richard Heinberg (Claireview Books, 2005)

During the oil crisis, civil disturbances may force the army out onto the streets to keep the peace.

## Communication disruption

Lack of transportation for deliveries and unreliable power sources mean that all lines of communication are frequently disrupted. People want to know what their government is doing to solve the crisis. At the same time, governments are using any channels possible to announce emergency measures such as curfews, rationing, car sharing, or the issuing of permits to travel.

## The army moves in

In the first few weeks of the crisis, there is a greater police presence in most places. However, the police have transportation issues of their own. It is obvious they cannot deal with rising fuel theft, carjackings, looting, and other social disturbances alone. Serious unrest requires military intervention. Riots in the French cities of Paris and Amiens mean the army has taken over disused buildings for security purposes. Other nations have the army on standby, in case of an emergency.

*"My father rode a camel. I drive a car. My son flies in a jet airplane. His son will ride a camel."*

A Saudi saying, taken from *The Party's Over: Oil, War and the Fate of Industrial Societies* by Richard Heinberg (Claireview Books, 2005)

In March 2012, Indonesian police clashed with protestors against the rise in fuel prices. Violent scenes like this could become common during the crisis.

# POWER OUTAGES

A month after the terrorist attack, interruptions to the power supply are reported from all over the world. But countries such as Poland and Taiwan are still able to generate a large proportion of electricity from coal-fired power stations because they have coal supplies.

People are asking why there is a problem if there is still so much coal in the ground. The problem is transporting the coal to power plants. And some countries are not exporting their coal, but rather keeping it for their own use.

## HOW IS ELECTRICITY GENERATED?

Electricity is generated in power stations. Fossil-fuel power stations burn coal, natural gas, or oil to produce electricity. Nuclear power is another nonrenewable source of energy. However, unlike fossil fuels, it is not likely to run out in the near future. Renewable power stations can be run on **hydropower**, solar heat, **geothermal heat**, and biomass.

In 2006, fossil fuels were still the most common fuels for electricity generation (see pie chart) worldwide.

Since the 1970s, scientists have warned that carbon dioxide from burning fossil fuels is causing global warming and climate change. Many governments have listened and are proposing to build more nuclear power stations while also encouraging investment in alternative energy sources.

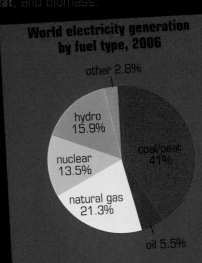

**World electricity generation by fuel type, 2006**

- other 2.8%
- hydro 15.9%
- coal/peat 41%
- nuclear 13.5%
- natural gas 21.3%
- oil 5.5%

## WHAT WOULD YOU DO?

### Home or export?

Norway has an abundance of renewable energy resources. In addition to hydropower, the country has invested in solar, wind, and biomass power. In wetter years, Norway has enough "clean" energy to export to neighboring countries such as Denmark. But during an energy crisis, Norway may choose to use more of that capacity for its own needs. In this situation, would you supply your own people or honor the contracts to your overseas customers?

# The energy winners

By 2020, many countries have already made a transition to renewable sources. These countries are set to handle the energy crisis better. Norway can generate over 99 percent of its own electricity needs from hydropower, although it usually sells some of this electricity to other countries. Iceland derives about three-quarters of its electricity from geothermal power.

In many areas, demand for electricity is outstripping supply. In some places, blackouts are a daily occurrence. This is having a serious impact on businesses and manufacturing. Some regions have implemented changes such as planned brownouts (a temporary drop in voltage to avoid a blackout, which can cause lights to dim and damage some electrical equipment) or rolling blackouts (a series of planned blackouts at different times over a geographical region). People are getting used to using less electricity. They keep flashlights and candles ready for when the electricity goes off. It is no surprise that there has been an increase in the number of domestic fires and accidents!

## GRID COLLAPSE

Electricity is generated at power stations and then distributed to users through transmission networks across a country known as **power grids**. These grid are interconnected and share power. So, if one power station is not working to capacity or has to temporarily shut down, electricity can be taken from another part of the grid. However, the grid would struggle to cope if many power stations were not operating to capacity or their output was not shared among different areas. When the grid cannot cope, there is a blackout!

The New York blackout in 2003 lasted over 24 hours and caused chaos to transportation, cell phone networks, water supplies, and industry.

# Global picture

Nations that began managing the transition from fossil fuels to low-energy, **sustainable** models earlier in the century are coping reasonably well in the crisis. Some rural communities in less-developed countries are also doing better, because they have always had a way of living that does not rely upon huge energy consumption. Industrial nations that refused to move with the times are the worst affected.

# Solar energy

Advances in solar power technology mean that many countries and communities have already built solar power stations or added **photovoltaic** installations to buildings and homes. Since the 1970s, solar power has worked well for small communities or people living in remote regions that are not connected to the power grid.

Small communities in sunny places such as Africa are adjusting to the crisis well. They suffer shortages of electricity on cloudy days but are learning to cut back when required. Residents of California have long embraced solar power and can boast more solar panels on homes than any other U.S. state. The development of solar power stations increased in the first decades of the 2000s. By 2020, industrial nations such as the United States, Germany, and Spain are well advanced in providing solar power. Developing nations such as China and India are also utilizing energy from the Sun.

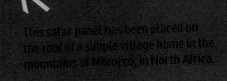

This solar panel has been placed on the roof of a simple village home in the mountains of Morocco, in North Africa.

# WHAT IS SOLAR POWER?

The Sun is Earth's major source of energy. Light and heat from the Sun sustain nearly all forms of life on the planet. Solar power is electricity generated via solar panels from sunlight. A solar panel contains groups of button-sized devices called solar cells. Light from the Sun causes electrons to jump between the cells to create a flow of electricity. Solar thermal power uses the Sun's energy to heat a liquid that is then used to generate steam and turn a turbine, generating electricity. The problem with solar power is how to store it so that it can be used during the nighttime or when the Sun is not shining. Scientists continue to investigate effective ways to store the Sun's heat.

↗

The Gujarat Solar Farm is a group of solar parks in northern India. In 2012, the park was proclaimed to be the biggest solar park in Asia. At this time, the park covered about 4,900 acres (about 2,000 hectares), with a generation capacity amounting to two-thirds of India's solar power production. In 2012, the Indian government announced plans to extend the park further into the desert.

# Nuclear power

Nuclear power is sustaining large-scale power grids in some places. Most stations are able to remain operational. Nuclear fuels are transported by rail in huge containers. Despite the upheaval of the railroad networks, governments everywhere have prioritized the transportation of nuclear fuels and the other goods needed to run the plants.

One major problem is how to dispose of **radioactive** waste safely. This is an expensive procedure that consumes large amounts of energy, but many governments have budgeted for the funds required. Nuclear power cannot pick up the slack when fossil-fueled power stations close down, but some governments are looking at their long-term nuclear programs again. They have halted decommissioning (the closure) of remaining plants and plan to develop more nuclear power stations in the future.

↗

In *the movie Mad Max 2: The Road Warrior* (1981), the world is plunged into chaos when oil begins to run out. In the future, can we expect the same thing to happen in real life?

In 2011, France was able to generate about 77 percent of its electricity from nuclear power. By 2020, this figure is even higher. The government has managed the situation by forcing cuts on domestic and industrial use. It has also set aside reserves of gasoline and diesel for the safe disposal of radioactive waste. It has been a sacrifice people have been happy to make.

# 1986 CHERNOBYL DISASTER

Nuclear power took off in the 1960s and 1970s. At this time, nuclear energy was praised as a cheap, pollution-free alternative to fossil fuels. Accidents such as the 1886 **Chernobyl disaster** in the Soviet Union made many more people question the safety of nuclear power. In 2011, after the accident at the Fukushima nuclear plant in Japan, Germany and Switzerland announced plans to phase out nuclear power stations. Nations such as Australia, Denmark, and Italy already opposed plans to develop nuclear power.

# Wind power

Nations that invested in wind power in the past are reaping the rewards now. The United States, the United Kingdom, China, Spain, Denmark, and Germany built up operations in the early 2000s. Turbines and wind farms already connected to the power grid are generating upward of one-quarter of the electricity supplied in some regions. Wind is an important resource during the crisis. In the past, many people complained about wind farms, claiming they ruined the appearance of landscapes. They blamed wind turbines at sea for killing wildlife. During the crisis, many people are not so quick to criticize this resource, and there is a rush to complete existing building projects.

# WHAT IS WIND POWER?

Humans have been using wind energy for thousands of years. Before the industrial age, windmills were the only way to grind grain other than by hand. The modern version of the windmill is the wind turbine. It needs wind to turn its blades and generate electricity. A wind farm is a group of wind turbines in the same place. Most wind farms are situated in open countryside or **offshore**, where there are no obstacles to wind flow.

Wind power is free, but the cost of building turbines and other infrastructure is high. Technical problems arise because the wind changes from day to day. This means wind power cannot be guaranteed to pick up the slack during a peak in energy demand. However, wind power has great potential, and scientists continue to research ways to harness and store wind power.

# Hydroelectricity

Hydroelectricity is another guarantee during the crisis. Some of the largest hydroelectric facilities in the world are in the United States, China, Brazil, and Venezuela. An oil crisis does not affect the flow of water, and these massive hydroelectric plants continue to operate to capacity. China invested in at least 15 major dam projects between 2012 and 2020, and many of these facilities are up and running and supplying electricity to China's growing industrial economy. A poor, less developed South American nation, Paraguay, is an unexpected winner. It produces all of its electricity from hydroelectric dams and exports its excess to Brazil and Argentina.

## "WHITE COAL"

Hydropower is often called "white coal" because of its abundance and potential power. In the 20th century, hydroelectric dams were built across many major rivers throughout the world. In 2012, water was still the most commonly used renewable resource for generating electricity. However, the potential for building more large dams is hampered by production costs and also by the negative impact on the environment.

In the future, there will be more run-of-the-river hydroelectric power stations. These plants are positioned next to rivers but do not require a large reservoir of stored water. Tidal power is another growth area, where the energy created by the tides of the sea is converted to power. Micro hydro plants using smaller rivers and streams will also become more common, as they are more practical and can be installed quickly.

# Electric solutions

It is a few months after the crisis began, and the world is still coming to terms with the disruption to the market in fossil fuels. International leaders, industrialists, and engineers gather daily to discuss how to get the most out of the resources they have.

They are also talking about long-term solutions for their countries. Experts are called in to give guidance and advice about energy resources. Politicians and businesses are now taking the advice about radical changes to energy policy much more seriously. In the past, they ignored inconvenient truths that would be unpopular with taxpayers and voters or cost their businesses. The options for each nation are very different. However, one thing is clear: most countries need to invest more money if they want the world to restore stability. And, at this time, money is tight. Many industries and businesses have gone bust and some financial markets look set to crash.

The Itaipu Dam on the Paraná River between Brazil and Paraguay was opened in 1984. It is the largest development of its kind in the world.

# FACT OR FICTION?

## Persuading leaders to make changes

"For an unnaturally large fee, he was to address an energy conference attended by institutional investors, pension-fund managers, solid types who would not be easily persuaded that the world, their world, was in danger and that they should align their investment patterns accordingly. Through inertia [lack of activity], blind professional custom, they were bound to their old familiars, oil, gas, coal, forestry. He was to persuade them that what they currently made profitable would one day destroy them."

Taken from *Solar* by Ian McEwan (Vintage, 2011). This novel is about a physicist on a quest to discover a solar energy solution to help prevent climate change.

# ONE YEAR LATER

One year later, the world remains a tense and unstable place. Many nations have economies that are suffering from the disruption to industry and trade. The tension between many nations rests on the issue of fuel supply. Some nations' energy supplies depend upon diplomatic relations with oil-rich nations in the Middle East or gas-rich nations such as Russia. Once upon a time, the most powerful nations in the world were the industrialized nations; now it is the countries that control energy supplies.

## HOW LIKELY IS IT?

### Would Russia withhold its energy supplies?

Russia holds the largest reserves of natural gas and is the leading producer and exporter of natural gas in the world. In 2006, Russia's dominant, state-run gas supplier, Gazprom, switched off its supply to neighboring Ukraine. Tensions had been high between Russia and the Ukraine for years. Ukrainians disputed paying more for natural gas than other European countries. Meanwhile, about 80 percent of natural gas destined for these European nations traveled through pipelines across the Ukraine. The situation became worse when the Russians accused the Ukrainians of diverting gas intended for other countries and using it for their own needs.

This crisis was swiftly resolved, but another major dispute erupted in 2008. On January 1, 2009, the dispute intensified and Russia cut off all supplies to Europe via the Ukrainian pipeline. Many eastern European domestic users were badly affected, because the shutdown came in the middle of a freezing-cold winter. Gas prices fluctuated throughout Europe. By January 21, gas supplies were resumed, but the crisis was a wake-up call to other European nations dependent upon Russian gas. In the event of a world energy crisis, Russia would probably react in the same way it did in 2009.

Food rationing means tight control of staples such as meat, dairy products, and legumes (foods like peas and beans). Here, lentils are being measured out for customers.

# Food crisis

Food has been running out. In the early days of the crisis, transporting goods was the problem, but there were stores of food that could be distributed, sometimes under government control. Now, the issue is food production. There is not enough oil to fuel tractors and other farming machinery, and the shortage has also severely affected the manufacture of pesticides and fertilizers that rely on oil. Without these artificial means of increasing crop yields, there are not enough crops for humans, let alone animals. As a result, there are fewer meat and dairy products available.

# Starvation

Food manufacturing and processing have been disrupted, and many businesses dealing with nonessential supplies have gone bust. With air transportation costs at a record high, some countries are critically hit because of a reliance on imported food. Demand for food has outstripped supply, and the price of food has skyrocketed. Governments that have not already introduced food rationing are now doing so.

Some people are trying to grow their own food. Soon, every available area of land is being planted, including gardens, parks, and football fields! However, the majority of people living in industrial societies are not prepared to grow enough food to supply their own needs. It takes years of readjustment and planning to resolve the problem. Not everyone has access to land—they rely on the good will and charity of others. Communities that band together are more successful. In the meantime, the quest to put food on our plates turns nasty. Food theft and scavenging are on the increase. Death from starvation, especially for the old and weak, is more common, too.

# Water supply

Maintaining a supply of water has also become a problem. Water treatment plants and pumping stations need energy. They also require maintenance and new components. Much of the water supply infrastructure is falling into disrepair, and many places can no longer rely upon safe, clean drinking water. Drinking untreated water can lead to deadly waterborne diseases such as cholera and dysentery.

Water conservation is another issue. Scientists have found that global warming is causing more frequent and severe droughts in some places around the world. Water management is key to keeping drought-stricken areas habitable (capable of being lived in). In the present crisis, desert cities such as Las Vegas and Los Angeles have become largely uninhabitable due to crippling shortages of water. People living next to lakes and rivers have a chance of survival, but water treatment is still a problem.

## FACT OR FICTION?

### Starved for moisture

"We lived...in a time of drought and war. The great empires had fallen and been divided. The land was parched and starved for moisture, and the men who lived on it fought for every drop. Outside, the wind howled like something wounded. Inside, our skin flaked, and our eyes stung and burned. Our tongues were like thick snakes asleep in dark graves."

Excerpt taken from *The Water Wars* by Cameron Stracher (Sourcebooks Fire, 2011)

# Health in crisis

The number of sick and dying has increased. Human life is more vulnerable than ever, but, at this time of great need, there is a decline in the standard of health care. Much modern medicine is dependent on oil. The main impact has been the transportation of drugs and other medical supplies. There are fewer emergency vehicles on the road. Many items, including synthetic rubber gloves and surgical instruments, are made using oil.

Meanwhile, hospitals need energy for heating, sterilization, and running medical equipment. Hospitals everywhere are prioritizing emergency and essential operations. Every country has its own health care system. In 2020, the countries that have already weaned themselves off oil dependency are in better shape.

# HOW LIKELY IS IT?

## Can hospitals cope with energy shortages?

In February 2012, the people of the Gaza Strip in the Middle East experienced the worst fuel shortage in years, caused by an Israeli **blockade**. At first, it was drivers who were hit. Then there were electric blackouts, and people in Gaza's hospitals suffered. Juan-Pedro Schaerer, the head of the International Committee of the Red Cross delegation for Israel and the territories, warned:

> "The current failure to ensure delivery of fuel and electricity could rapidly lead to interruptions in vital public services such as hospital care and water supply, putting the lives of thousands of patients in danger…in the event of any such disruption, hospital operating rooms and specialist units, such as those providing intensive care, neonatal care, and dialysis, would be especially hard hit."

In May 2012, there were reports of deaths and injuries caused by the fuel shortage. The crisis is, to date, ongoing.

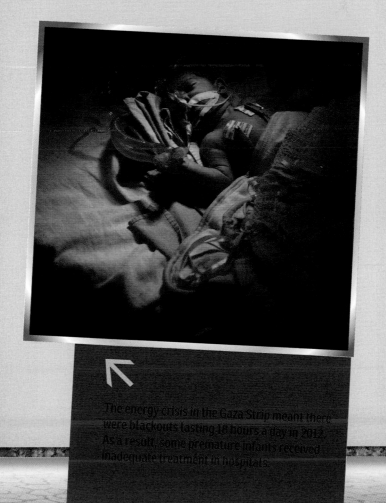

The energy crisis in the Gaza Strip meant there were blackouts lasting 18 hours a day in 2012. As a result, some premature infants received inadequate treatment in hospitals.

# The survivors

Who are the survivors of a society in turmoil? In some places, the black market for food and fuel helps to cater to those who can afford it. People living in the slums of developing countries or poor farmers in remote parts of Africa, Asia, and South America are coping better. These people have lived more sustainable lives than city dwellers for years. They have lots of small, adaptable businesses that do not rely upon electricity. Carpenters use hand tools rather than power tools. Farmers till the land using animals rather than tractors.

Born into poverty, many of these people know how to survive on very little. They do not waste food and they recycle and reuse everything. These age-old skills have been passed down to them through generations and are serving them well during the energy crisis.

A boy in Calcutta, India, makes a dollar a day by collecting empty plastic bottles and taking them to a recycling plant. Plastic bottles become more valuable during the crisis.

# Fossil-free cities

In the 2000s, some countries and regions planned for a fossil-free future and adapted their lives to be more eco-conscious. In 2020, many of these places are reaping the rewards of their forward planning. Such places already have power plants run on biomass or other renewable resources. They have solar installations on rooftops and roadsides to generate electricity and heat. Wind turbines are generating enough energy to power public buildings such as hospitals. High-efficiency transit systems such as monorails run on electricity have replaced fuel-guzzling trains and buses. Some places have wider cycle paths and limits on car use in urban areas.

Meanwhile, some places have urban farms supplying citizens with locally produced food. In some towns, small businesses and stores have been built specifically to be a cycle-ride or walking distance away from these homes. No place is immune to the energy crisis, but these cities and communities are more able to maintain a reasonable standard of living. These places are becoming the **template** for most of the world post-fossil fuels.

## HOW LIKELY IS IT?

### Fossil-free cities

Becoming a fossil-free city is not easy, but it is already happening today. It takes years of planning and a change in thinking. The city of Växjö in Sweden converted its local power plant from oil to biomass in 1979. In 1996, the city pledged to become free of fossil fuels by 2030. Its three-pronged attack included energy conservation, the development of renewable energy, and changing the habits of its citizens.

The city has the advantage of being surrounded by forests and lakes. Waste from the forest industry is burned at the local power plant to generate heat and power. Currently, 90 percent of the energy used to heat the city and half of its electricity is derived from trees. In the past, the lakes around Växjö were badly polluted. Today, the sewage treatment plant pumps clean water into the lakes and converts sludge from the dirty water to biogas.

In the future, the city hopes to run its buses on locally produced biogas. In 2007, it was reported that Växjö was "Europe's greenest city." Växjö's success relies upon careful urban planning, but it also requires people to take responsibility in their everyday lives. Initiatives include installing devices that allow people to monitor their water, heat, and electricity consumption.

# The world in 2020

This map shows some of the major events involved in our fictional energy crisis. Some countries remain relatively unaffected because they are rich in energy; others are suffering huge disruptions to their way of life. Around the world, pollution levels have decreased, since fewer fossil fuels are being burned. Without so many airplanes, the skies are quieter. Some experts are even claiming that the crisis might be a blessing in disguise for the future of the planet.

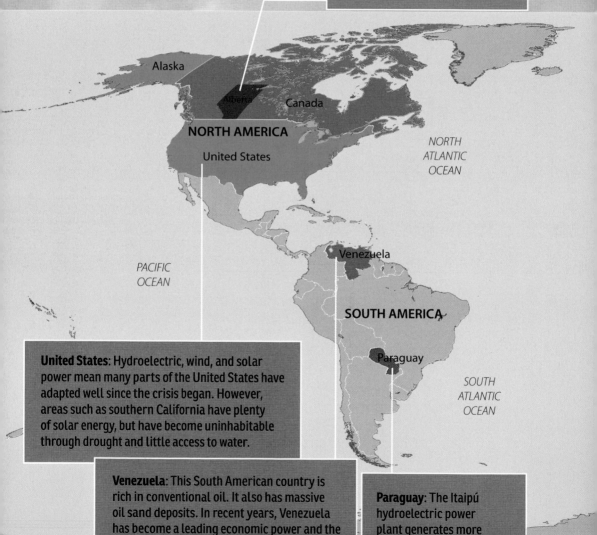

**Canada**: Canada has plenty of untapped oil within the oil sands in the province of Alberta.

Alaska

Alberta

Canada

**NORTH AMERICA**

United States

NORTH ATLANTIC OCEAN

PACIFIC OCEAN

Venezuela

**SOUTH AMERICA**

Paraguay

SOUTH ATLANTIC OCEAN

**United States**: Hydroelectric, wind, and solar power mean many parts of the United States have adapted well since the crisis began. However, areas such as southern California have plenty of solar energy, but have become uninhabitable through drought and little access to water.

**Venezuela**: This South American country is rich in conventional oil. It also has massive oil sand deposits. In recent years, Venezuela has become a leading economic power and the chief supplier of oil to the United States.

**Paraguay**: The Itaipú hydroelectric power plant generates more hydroelectric power than any other hydroelectric power station in the world.

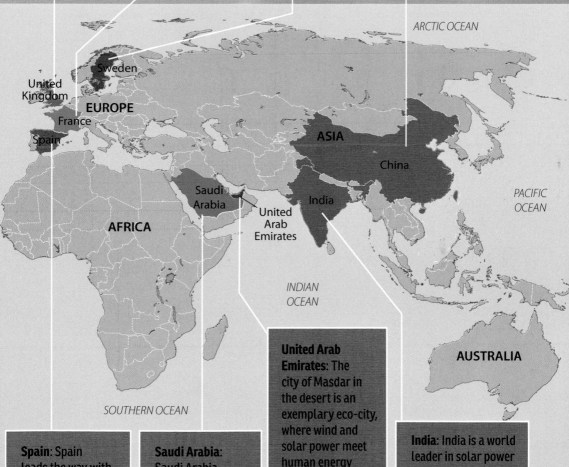

**France**: France's long-standing nuclear-energy program means it still produces more nuclear power than any other nation. Slovakia, Switzerland, Belgium, and Hungary are also top producers.

**United Kingdom**: The UK uses offshore wind power.

**Sweden**: The fossil-free city of Växjö in Sweden has become the template for sustainable cities all over the world.

**China**: China remains a top industrial nation because it has made a successful transition to renewable energy while also maintaining some of its large coal-fired power stations. The Three Gorges Dam on the Yangtze is the second-largest hydroelectric power complex in the world.

ARCTIC OCEAN

Sweden

United Kingdom

EUROPE

France

Spain

ASIA

China

PACIFIC OCEAN

Saudi Arabia

United Arab Emirates

India

AFRICA

INDIAN OCEAN

AUSTRALIA

SOUTHERN OCEAN

**Spain**: Spain leads the way with solar power in Europe. It exports a percentage of its output to Germany.

**Saudi Arabia**: Saudi Arabia remains powerful because of its oil and gas reserves.

**United Arab Emirates**: The city of Masdar in the desert is an exemplary eco-city, where wind and solar power meet human energy requirements. Even though the country is oil rich, the cars in this city are powered by magnets.

**India**: India is a world leader in solar power and wind power. Solar power plants commissioned back in 2011/12 now supply nearly half of the nation's needs.

# THE NEW WAY OF LIFE

It is five years since the crisis started, and some places have become uninhabitable. Millions of people have migrated in search of better lives. Journeys are not easy. Many roads have fallen into disrepair. Meanwhile, journeys overseas are long and expensive, although still viable using wind power. Countries that had managed the transition to renewable resources and cities that had modeled themselves on successful fossil-free cities have become popular escapes. Some governments have responded to the new migration by shutting down borders or imposing stricter immigration laws.

## Acceptance

Millions of people have accepted the changed circumstances and remained in their communities. They are learning to live with less energy and to build their lives around the changes. These days, they are happy with enough food to survive, and there are a lot fewer obese people. People do not expect to be able to eat foods that cannot be produced locally.

In the same way, most people do not expect to fill their homes with electrical appliances and the latest must-have gadgets. Now that it is difficult and expensive to travel long distances, people are enjoying leisure time closer to home. This is bringing people and communities together. Some people even say that the change has been for the best!

Smaller communities have realized that the only way to survive is to make life more sustainable. In a less mobile world, it is essential for local communities to pull together. People have to share their skills and resources. Food production is crucial, and many people have relearned basic skills. At first, it was a challenge to make bread. Now the bread-making process starts with tilling the land and sowing the grain.

## FACT OR FICTION?

### A loaf of bread

"'Look what I shot,' Gale holds up a loaf of bread with an arrow stuck in it, and I laugh. It's real bakery bread, not the flat, dense loaves we make from our grain rations. I take it in my hands, pull out the arrow, and hold the puncture in the crust to my nose, inhaling the fragrance that makes my mouth flood with saliva."

From THE HUNGER GAMES by Suzanne Collins, Scholastic Inc./Scholastic Press. Copyright © 2008 by Suzanne Collins. Reproduced by permission.

Experienced farmers lend their knowledge. After harvesting, the grain is ground to make flour. The skills of trained engineers, carpenters, and builders have been called upon to build modern windmills. Finally, experienced bakers have had the job of making bread. By pulling together and working as a team, people have found the manpower, tools, and machinery they need for the basic processing of food.

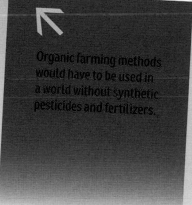

Organic farming methods would have to be used in a world without synthetic pesticides and fertilizers.

# Farming and Foraging

Communities are farming with limited machinery and without synthetic pesticides and fertilizers. The fit and able work in the fields during sowing and harvest time. Many communities are growing fruits and vegetables. People are also adapting their diets. They are foraging for wild food such as mushrooms, herbs, and berries. People are also hunting for animals or go fishing. In some places, this is threatening the survival of species, as some animals and birds are being hunted to extinction.

# Housing

By 2025, most people have made their homes more sustainable. Communities and countries that developed energy-efficient passive buildings earlier in the century are doing better. Some places have whole housing programs, schools, stores, and hospitals utilizing energy from the Sun. Meanwhile, many others cannot afford the new technology. As in the past, most governments are offering advice about **insulation**, and there are programs to help people reduce energy consumption and install solar systems. In reality, millions of people are still living in cold or underheated buildings.

These passive solar houses in Germany may be how our homes of the future will look.

# Around the home

New technology such as solar ovens and refrigerators run on biomass are replacing electric ovens and traditional refrigerators in some homes. Many cannot afford these new appliances, and production cannot easily meet demand. In some communities, people have to share cooking on open fires or old-fashioned stoves that burn wood or coal. As a result, many areas of woodland are under threat. In some places, wood smoke is causing pollution and there are reports of smog.

## WHAT WOULD YOU DO?

### Daily living needs

Imagine yourself living in 2025 without the money to add solar panels to your home. What would you use to heat your home in the winter? What would you do to make food? Would you try to work with other people in the community to meet your daily living requirements?

Passive homes and buildings are designed to have low energy needs. They have better insulation and an efficient ventilation system. They are designed to use the Sun's heat. For this reason, windows are positioned on the south-facing side of the building, while a sloped roof is built on the north side of the building, to reduce heat loss. Meanwhile, solar panels on the roof and walls collect heat to be used in the house.

In 2012, more than 37,000 passive houses were estimated to exist worldwide, a tiny fraction of total housing. European countries such as Germany, Switzerland, Denmark, and Sweden are leaders in the field, but passive housing is becoming popular in other countries. By 2025, some governments might require buildings to follow this standard.

Many people are using alternative food preservation techniques such as salting, pickling, or drying food. Waste management has become part of everyday life. Many more homes have **composters** under the sink and composter toilets; the compost is used in their own yards or on community farms. People are throwing away less and reusing precious resources such as paper and glass. Anything that cannot be reused is recycled.

## Virtual lives

While, generally speaking, people are simplifying the way they live, others are more reliant on new technology than ever. Limited transportation is pushing them toward virtual living. Electricity is not a thing of the past, so computers and other technology can still be used. However, electricity is more expensive and less reliable. This is frustrating at a time when more people than ever are working from home using computers and video conferencing.

In the future, energy from the Sun will be used to charge cell phones and other gadgets.

# Industry and manufacturing

Many of the changes to everyday living have depended upon how industry has adapted during the crisis. At the beginning of the crisis, transportation disruptions led to the closure of many factories. People had less money and became more accustomed to reuse. The market forces of supply and demand drove many more manufacturers out of business, especially if they produced luxury goods. The petrochemical and petroplastic industries were reliant on oil, so they are now smaller and are under strict government control.

# Economic growth

The demand for passive housing and new energy-efficient technology has grown. Some new ventures have been able to organize the money, resources, and energy to supply these needs—often with the help of governments. In many countries, the manufacturing sector has revived. However, much of the new growth in the economy is from smaller local businesses, which are far more energy-conscious than before. There are also more products made from renewable resources or recycled materials. One growth area is bioplastics.

# Energy around us

Inventors and scientists are coming up with new ways to generate energy and to make the best of limited resources. Some of the most bizarre ideas for generating energy actually work very well. Some gyms have hooked up to **generators**. All that running on treadmills, riding exercise bikes, and using rowing machines is being converted to electricity. Meanwhile, some crematoriums are converting the heat generated from burning corpses to electricity or using it to heat buildings.

## HOW LIKELY IS IT?
### Bioplastics made from chicken feathers

Bioplastics can be made from plant-based oils such as soybeans, hemp, corn, and pea starch. Bioplastics are cheaper to make than petroplastics and are **biodegradable**. Currently, bioplastics are not as strong or durable as petroplastics, but scientists are making advances all the time. One of the most exciting developments recently has been bioplastic from chicken feathers. Researchers at the University of Nebraska's Institute of Agriculture and Natural Resources have developed a plastic that is strong enough to be used for car bumpers and durable enough to make cell phone cases.

↙

Post-2020, people will find more unusual ways to light up city streets. In 2010, a gas light in a park in Massachusetts is powered by the methane gas that is given off from dog waste!

## The new spirit

Everyday life for many people is getting back on track. With societies and communities pulling together, there is a new spirit of survival. People are also finding ways to entertain themselves in a world that has changed so much. They have been forced to seek out simpler pleasures. There is a renaissance of the arts and more appreciation of the natural world. In some places, there has been a total backlash against technology. Rather than tuning into iPods, people are rediscovering live music. There is more focus on personal fitness. People are valuing their possessions and cherishing each other more. Many people look back in horror at the **consumerism** and throwaway culture of the 20th century. Together, they are building a stronger, better, more sustainable future.

### WHAT WOULD YOU DO?

#### Entertainment

Picture yourself in this new world in 2025. Imagine that you do not have the gadgets and electronic equipment that you take for granted now. What talents, skills, and hobbies would you fall back on? Do you think you would still enjoy yourself?

# WHAT CAN WE DO?

In this book, we have presented some possible consequences of people struggling to cope with a shortage of oil and other fossil fuels. Some experts believe that we have already reached peak oil—which might suggest, although nobody knows for certain, that we have 20 years before we begin to run out. If this is the case, shouldn't everyone be doing more now to make our lives more sustainable?

## Is there a problem?

Some scientists and politicians argue that we will not run out of oil in the immediate future. They say there are oil reserves that have not been discovered yet. They think we have made advances in drilling techniques that make it possible to extract oil that we could not reach before. Some experts believe there is enough shale oil to last us thousands of years, but at the moment the cost of extraction is still too high. Oil sands are another potential source that is not economically viable yet. Other experts believe that extracting shale oil and oil sands is too damaging to the environment.

There is an international consensus and overwhelming scientific evidence that our consumption of fossil fuels is causing global warming. Many scientists and experts predict that extreme weather conditions caused by global warming will plunge the world into an environmental crisis. If we continue to burn fossil fuels at the same rate, they believe the environmental crisis might happen before we run out of fossil fuels. They think we should reduce the consumption of fossil fuels for the sake of the planet and human society.

Large reserves of oil sands are currently known to exist in Canada (seen here), Kazakhstan, and Russia.

# Action plan

How would you cope if there were an oil crisis? What could you do now to prepare for such an event? Here are a few ideas:

- Travel by bus, train, or bike or walk more. You are getting to the age when you may be thinking about getting a car. Remember to choose smaller, more fuel-efficient cars.

- Reduce your carbon footprint by not buying as many new products that you do not need, such as gadgets and clothes. They all require energy to manufacture and distribute.

- Reduce your energy consumption. Think about switching off lights and not leaving your computer and other gadgets on standby.

- Find out more about alternative energies such as wind power and solar power. The more you know, the more you can tell other people and try to influence their decisions.

- Grow your own food. You can do this at home or school.

- Consume less and remember the three "Rs": reduce, reuse, recycle!

- Get handy! The more you can do yourself, the less you will need to use electricity! Learn new skills such as sewing by hand or carpentry.

- Get involved! Find out about environmental groups that are active in your community. Join groups and sign petitions that help to bring about change.

"History demonstrates that the deepest and most meaningful cultural/social/political changes began with individuals, not organizations, governments, or institutions."

The Last Hours of Ancient Sunlight by Thom Hartmann (Mobius, 2001)

"We must face the prospect of changing our basic ways of living. This change will either be made on our own initiative in a planned way, or forced on us with chaos and suffering by the inexorable laws of nature."

Jimmy Carter, speaking in 1976, shortly before he became U.S. president, from The Party's Over: Oil, War and the Fate of Industrial Societies by Richard Heinberg (Claireview Books, 2005)

# Making the transition

The Transition Movement is based on the idea that local communities need to make a gradual, carefully planned transition toward a fossil-free future. This means looking at every sector of a community, including food, trade, the local economy, housing, heating, education, health, and waste management. It means making plans for a more sustainable future. Some communities have decided to take responsibility and have joined the Transition Movement. Their action plans include raising awareness, forming work groups and sharing skills, creating sustainable projects in their towns, building relationships with the local governments, and creating an action plan to reduce energy use.

Get a skill or a trade! You can learn some tricks of the trade like these volunteers on a construction site in New York.

## THE FIRST TRANSITION TOWN

Totnes, in Devon, England, is no ordinary town. In 2005, it became the first Transitional Town in the world. The people of Totnes aim to become less dependent on fossil fuels and to reduce carbon emissions, while strengthening the local economy and becoming more self-reliant in producing food, energy, and services. Initiatives include turning the town's parking lot into a garden and installing solar panels on civic buildings. Totnes has become the model for transitional initiatives all around the world. It may well set the template for how we should live in the future.

# The Future

Nobody knows for certain what will happen in the world after fossil fuels run out. We cannot even be sure when or if it will happen. In this book, we have explored what could happen in an oil crisis and the domino effect this could have on the use of fossil fuels. It is unlikely that we will completely run out of fossil fuels in the near future, but the clock is ticking, and governments around the world are seeking alternative energy solutions.

Technology holds the key. Some scientists believe nuclear fusion is the key to a limitless supply of clean energy. Others think the answer lies out in space: one day it may be possible to source nuclear fuel from the Moon or have space-based solar power stations. Even further into the future, when fossil fuels are depleted, will there be human colonization of space? Plans for space tourism exist now—will this lead to permanent space colonies? Some of these ideas may sound like science fiction, but sci-fi predictions often have a way of coming true.

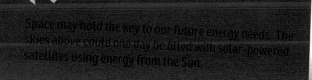

Space may hold the key to our future energy needs. The skies above could one day be filled with solar-powered satellites using energy from the Sun.

# WRITE YOUR OWN STORY

You may have already thought about a world after fossil fuels, or it may be an entirely new idea to you. A world like this has been described by many writers, and you could write your own view of how people would live in a world without fossil fuels.

## Inspiration

First, you will need inspiration. This simple exercise will soon get the creative juices flowing: think about the countless ways that gasoline or oil affects your life.

You may start off with basics such as the clothes on your back and the food you eat. How would an oil crisis affect the supply of food and clothes? Very soon, you may be asking questions such as: "What would I do if there were no more essentials left at my local store?" Imagine what you would do in this scenario. What would other people do? Describe some possible outcomes. Expand your scenario to include other aspects of daily life, such as school, work, health, and entertainment.

## Research

Over the next few weeks, make sure you take a notepad out with you. Hopefully, new ideas will come to you when you are going about your daily life. Talk to friends and family about the subject and jot down any interesting ideas. Watch the world around you and write down your observations. Read about the subject and begin to research your ideas. Try to understand how much technology relies on fossil fuels and the potential difficulties and pitfalls of relying on certain types of technology.

Delve into fiction, nonfiction, and magazine and newspaper articles and browse the Internet. Watch movies or television shows about world crises. If you absorb all kinds of information, it will help to shape your story.

## The plot

Once you have an idea for your story, you may be tempted to start writing. However, it is a good idea to write a plot and plan the basics of the story. A good plot needs an introduction, action, a climatic event, and a conclusion. You may have a great idea for an ending, but you don't know how to start the story. Don't let this stop you from moving forward with writing the plot. Let your imagination go to work, but always have the plot in mind.

## Background information

A good story needs strong settings. A story after fossil fuels runs out will probably be set in the future. Think about how far into the future this is going to be. A book set in the immediate future needs to feel realistic in the situations, technology, and behavior of the people it describes. The notes you kept will come in handy for this. If the book is set hundreds of years from now, your imagination can go wild. However, write down as much of the background information as possible, so that when you begin writing your story it will be consistent.

## Characters

Interesting characters are key to a good read. The conflict between the "heroes" and the "bad guys" often drives a good story, but try to make it believable. Make a character list before you begin, noting personality traits, appearances, backgrounds, and relationships. You may not include all this in the story, but it will help you to get to know the characters before you start writing.

Once you have as much background as possible, then start writing. That first page is crucial. Work on it until you are sure you have a gripping introduction. From there, let the plot guide the way and allow your imagination to do the rest. Writing is not easy, so don't give up. Good luck!

# TIMELINE

**March 16, 2020**
Car bombs are detonated in Riyadh, Saudi Arabia, killing 30 people

**March 19, 2020**
Suicide bombers kill hundreds of Westerners and Saudis living in Riyadh, Saudi Arabia

**March 20, 2020**
Terrorists begin attacking oil tankers in the Strait of Hormuz in the Persian Gulf

**March 21, 2020– September 2020**
Terrorists make surprise attacks against oil tankers in the Persian Gulf, bringing the export of oil from the Gulf to non-Arabic nations to a virtual standstill

**March 21, 2020**
Large lines at gas stations are reported all around the world. Certain news reports suggest there is a "Global Oil Crisis," while other news sources urge people not to panic buy fuel.

**March 21, 2020**
Emergency talks are held in government offices around the world to figure out the severity of the situation

**March 24, 2020**
There are reports of gas stations running out of gasoline because of panic buying. World leaders begin crisis talks to avoid actual oil shortages. People begin panic buying staples such as bread. Airlines cancel flights; most flights are delayed.

**April 4, 2020**
Gasoline becomes a scarce resource and more than quadruples in price in most places. Fuel fury and fuel theft are on the increase. Protests are held outside government buildings and oil refineries around the world.

**April 5, 2020**
Traffic organizations report a decrease in the number of vehicles on the roads. Trucks are unable to deliver goods. In a poll in the United States, over half of corporations suggest that less than 50 percent of their workforce is able to make the commute to work.

**April 6, 2020**
Serious food shortages at supermarkets and food outlets mean that some governments are forced to introduce emergency measures such as the rationing of staple foods

**April 10, 2020**
Less than a month after the crisis started, some governments have introduced curfews to maintain public order

**April 11, 2020**
Airlines are at a standstill apart from emergency traffic. Trains carrying goods and passengers are canceled or providing very limited service. Undelivered cargo is piling up at airports and railroad stations.

**April 20, 2020**
Small and large businesses are struggling to cope in the crisis, and many have gone out of business, causing more shortages

## April 21, 2020

Power outages and blackouts are reported in most countries, as some wide-ranging power grids struggle to cope

## June 2020

Government leaders work around the clock to find a way to handle the energy crisis long term. Many leaders understand that they need to invest in more nonrenewable energy sources.

## 2021

The world is in economic meltdown, and many nations face economic collapse. Industry and manufacturing are in crisis.

Oil-rich nations in the Middle East, Russia, and China are coping much better.

Food production is in crisis, and nations that previously relied upon imported staple foodstuffs have greater shortages. More nations are introducing food rationing to help manage the situation.

The supply of safe, clean drinking water is an issue around the world. Desert cities like Las Vegas and Los Angeles have become virtual ghost towns because of water shortages.

Health services around the globe are seriously disrupted. Many hospitals are prioritizing emergency treatment.

Fossil-free cities that have developed sustainable ways of living, such as Växjö in Sweden, have become the template for developments around the world.

## 2025

The makeup of countries around the world change as millions of people migrate to different countries or areas that have managed the transition to renewable resources and adapt their lifestyles.

Everyday life changes for everyone: consumerism is a thing of the past. Many families do not have a vehicle; they use bicycles or rely upon public transportation networks. There is more acceptance of the situation, and people do not expect life to return to normal. Rather, they are making new lives for themselves.

Many small communities around the world are successfully feeding themselves and sustaining their communities.

For industry and manufacturing, the focus is now on energy-efficient technology.

Social commentators call this the "New Age"—it is a time of innovation and community spirit.

# GLOSSARY

**anaerobic digester** method of breaking down and treating biodegradable waste without the need for oxygen. Microorganisms break down the waste into a nutrient-rich organic matter that can be used to improve soil.

**biodegradable** able to rot away over time

**biofuel** fuel made from plants

**biomass** plant material or animal waste that is burned to create energy

**black market** illegal trading of rationed goods or goods that are very rare

**blockade** prevents something, such as fuel, from entering or exiting an area—for example, a harbor or oil refinery

**carbon dioxide** gas that is given off when fossil fuels, such as coal, oil, and natural gas, are burned. It is called a greenhouse gas because it traps heat from the Sun in Earth's atmosphere and adds to the greenhouse effect.

**Chernobyl disaster** accident at the Chernobyl nuclear power station in the Soviet Union on April 25, 1986. The fire and explosion at the plant caused radioactive material to be released into the atmosphere. The impact of the accident is debated, but about 19 miles (31 kilometers) around the plant remain an exclusion zone over 25 years after the disaster.

**composter** container in which waste vegetable matter is collected and converted to compost

**consumerism** overattachment to material possessions that leads to greater spending and consumption of goods

**crude oil** oil as it is found naturally underground

**curfew** regulation requiring people to remain indoors between certain hours

**diesel** fuel obtained from crude oil that is similar to gasoline

**generator** machine that turns the energy of movement into electricity

**geologist** professional person who studies the geological features of Earth

**geothermal heat** heat from deep underground, such as hot springs

**global warming** rise in the average temperature of Earth's atmosphere

**hydropower** electricity that is generated from the energy of running water, usually by a power station built on a dam across a river

**Industrial Revolution** rapid development of industry in Europe and North America during the late 18th and 19th centuries, brought about by the introduction of machinery, steam power, and the growth of factories

**insulation** protective layers of material used to trap heat and prevent it from escaping

**nonrenewable resource** resource that cannot be replaced

**offshore** in the sea not far from the coast

**oil refinery** industrial plant where oil is processed and purified

**OPEC (Organization of the Petroleum Exporting Countries)** organization created in 1960 that included the nations of Iran, Iraq, Kuwait, and Saudi Arabia. Since then, other members have included Qatar, Libya, Algeria, and Nigeria. The organization's objectives include coordinating and unifying policies on petroleum to secure fair and stable prices for its members.

**photovoltaic** relating to the generation of electricity from the Sun

**power grid** network of electric power lines

**radioactive** emits harmful radiation rays

**renewable resource** source of energy, such as water, wind, or solar power, that can never be used up

**scarcity** when goods are in short supply and cannot meet demand

**sustainable** something that can be maintained without depleting natural resources

**template** something that is a model or guide for others to copy

# FIND OUT MORE

## Nonfiction books

Challoner, Jack. *Energy* (DK Eyewitness). New York: Dorling Kindersley, 2012.

Gorman, Jacqueline Laks. *Fossil Fuels* (What If We Do Nothing?). Pleasantville, N.Y.: Gareth Stevens, 2009.

Morris, Neil. *Fossil Fuels* (Energy Now and in the Future). Mankato, Minn.: Smart Apple Media, 2007.

Thomas, Isabel. *The Pros and Cons of Biomass Power* (Energy Debate). New York: Rosen Central, 2008.

## Fiction books

Bacigalupi, Paolo. *Ship Breaker*. New York: Little, Brown, 2010.

Dickinson, Peter. *The Changes: The Weathermonger*. Boston: Little, Brown, 1969.

McCarthy, Cormac. *The Road*. New York: Alfred A. Knopf, 2006.

Stracher, Cameron. *The Water Wars*. Naperville, Ill.: Sourcebooks Fire, 2011.

## Web sites

**energy.gov/science-innovation/energy-sources/renewable-energy/solar**
Learn more about solar energy on the U.S. Department of Energy web site.

**www.greenenergychoice.com/green-guide/fossil-fuels.html**
This site is full of information about how our consumption of fossil fuels affects the environment.

**www.greenpeace.org/usa/en/campaigns/global-warming-and-energy**
Greenpeace advises people about the dangers of global warming.

**www.nature.org/greenliving/carboncalculator/index.htm**
Use this calculator to figure out your carbon footprint.

**www.windpoweringamerica.gov**
This U.S. Department of Energy web site has lots of information about the possibilities of wind power.

# Topics to research

## Design a car of the future

Research and design your own vehicle of the future. Explore different ideas such as solar-powered cars or vehicles that utilize magnets for motion. Investigate the kinds of vehicles that are already being designed and presented at car shows now. Play with ideas and think about different ways to generate the energy to power cars. Think about energy efficiency and how this car would operate in a world after fossil fuels run out.

Next, think about the design of the car and the features it will need to make it even more efficient. The final step is to design the vehicle. You could do this on paper or on a computer. This is an activity you may enjoy at home, but it could work well in class as a group activity, too. At school there would be more opportunities for group discussion and evaluating the different designs. Making a model of the car would be a great extension of this activity.

## Businesses of the future

Imagine yourself living in a world after fossil fuels. What kinds of jobs and careers will people have? How will workers make a living? What types of businesses will there be? The world will be a much more uncertain place. Think about the jobs and skills that you would need in this situation.

If you were to set up your own enterprise or business, what would it be? Why do you think it would work, and how would you start up this business? Is your idea realistic, and could it make money? What would the risks be, and how would you make your business succeed? This would make a good group activity that allows you to explore ideas together. Once you have discussed and investigated your ideas, write a business plan.

# INDEX